What I Know

I KNOW POSITION WORDS

By Rosie Banks

Gareth Stevens
PUBLISHING

first concepts

I know where
things are!
The moon is above
the water.

The girl is under the table.

The rabbit is beside the dog.

The pencil is on top of the book.

The cat is inside the box.

The horse is outside the barn.

The cow is behind the fence.

The flag is in front of the school.

The boy is next to
the bike.

The squirrel is between the flowers.

Point to the cookies outside the jar.

Love
Love

Please visit our website, www.garethstevens.com. For a free color catalog of all our high-quality books, call toll free 1-800-542-2595 or fax 1-877-542-2596.

Library of Congress Cataloging-in-Publication Data

Names: Banks, Rosie, author.
Title: I know position words / Rosie Banks.
Description: New York : Gareth Stevens Publishing, [2019] | Series: What I know | Includes index.
Identifiers: LCCN 2017040803| ISBN 9781538217429 (library bound) | ISBN 9781538217443 (paperback) | ISBN 9781538217450 (6 pack)
Subjects: LCSH: English language–Vocabulary–Juvenile literature. | English language–Nominals. | English language–Grammatical catagories.
Classification: LCC PE1449 .B3244 2018 | DDC 428.1–dc23 LC record available at https://lccn.loc.gov/2017040803

Published in 2019 by
Gareth Stevens Publishing
111 East 14th Street, Suite 349
New York, NY 10003

Designer: Bethany Perl
Editor: Therese Shea

Photo credits: Cover, p. 1 (stripes) Eky Studio/Shutterstock.com; cover, p. 1 (seesaw) Zynatis/Shutterstock.com; p. 3 Galyna Andrushko/Shutterstock.com; p. 5 Klaus Vedfelt/DigitalVision/Getty Images; p. 7 Eric Isselee/Shutterstock.com; p. 9 korkeng/Shutterstock.com; p. 11 Konstantin Askenov/Shutterstock.com; p. 13 debra millet/Shutterstock.com; p. 15 Heath Johnson/Shutterstock.com; p. 17 Pete Spiro/Shutterstock.com; p. 19 Petr Bonek/Shutterstock.com; p. 21 geertweggen/Shutterstock.com; p. 23 Africa Studio/Shutterstock.com.

Printed in the United States of America

CPSIA compliance information: Batch #CS18GS: For further information contact Gareth Stevens, New York, New York at 1-800-542-2595.